UP THE GARDEN PATH

UP THE GARDEN PATH

thelwell's
GUIDE TO GARDENING

EYRE METHUEN

First published in 1967
by Methuen & Co Ltd
11 *New Fetter Lane, London EC4*
Reprinted 1971
First published in this edition 1972
Reprinted 1973
Printed Offset Litho in Great Britain by
Cox & Wyman Ltd, Fakenham, Norfolk
SBN 413 29370 X

CONTENTS

TECHNICAL TERMS
EXPLAINED

SUCKERS

EARTHING UP

CLUB ROOT

GARDEN FENCING

MITES

BLACK SPOT

FREEZIA

HARDY ANNUALS

TOP DRESSING

SNOW IN
SUMMER

PHLOX

STONE CROP

PESTICIDE

GARDEN ROLLER

A HEAVY CROPPER

DAMPING OFF

GARDEN TALK

" I'VE DECIDED TO DO SOME MUCK SPREADING. "

" IT RAN AMOK."

" I THINK I'VE FOUND

YOUR TRANSISTOR RADIO"

" EVERY DAMN POTATO'S A FREAK . "

" WHO TURNED THE PRESSURE UP? "

" THEY'RE CREOSOTING
    THE FENCE NEXT DOOR. "

" I TOLD YOU THAT
    HANGING BASKET WAS LOOSE "

" ... AND THEN, BEYOND THE LAWNS, A LILY POOL WITH FOUNTAIN
AND A ROSE PERGOLA LEADING TO A RUSTIC SUMMER HOUSE . . . ."

" THAT WAS A STUPID PLACE TO PUT THE LAWN MOWINGS. "

" YOU NEVER LIKED THAT CONCRETE GNOME, DID YOU ? "

" I'M LETTING IT LIE FALLOW THIS YEAR. "

" DO YOU MIND IF A FEW REPORTERS COME THROUGH ?"

" IS THAT WHAT WE PAY HIM SEVENTY PENCE AN HOUR FOR ? "

" YOU GIVE UP TOO EASILY, DEAR . "

" WE CLIMBED THREE THOUSAND FEET
UP MONT BLANC TO GET THAT ONE "

" YOU'VE GOT YOUR FOOT ON MY SHALLOTS, MATE. "

FRIENDS & NEIGHBOURS

A GIVE-AND-TAKE RELATIONSHIP WITH YOUR NEIGHBOUR IS ESSENTIAL
TO THE FULL ENJOYMENT OF YOUR GARDEN

NEVER CRITICISE HIS CREATIVE EFFORTS ...

OR INSIST ON GIVING HIM UNSOLICITED ADVICE

WHEN HE IS IN TROUBLE, BE PREPARED TO HELP OUT OF COURSE

IF HIS ANIMALS SHOULD STRAY — LET HIM KNOW BY ALL MEANS

BUT DON'T BE VINDICTIVE

AVOID CONSTANT BORROWING

A HOUSEHOLDER IS ENTITLED TO REMOVE ANY OBJECT
        THAT ENCROACHES ON HIS PROPERTY –

BUT IT **MUST** BE RETURNED TO THE RIGHTFUL OWNER

MAKING A SPLASH

FOR THOSE WHO HAVE NOT TRIED IT BEFORE
WATER GARDENING CAN BE GREAT FUN

SOME PEOPLE GET PLEASURE

FROM WORKING OUT AMBITIOUS SCHEMES

OTHERS PREFER THE MODERN, EASY WAY

A FOUNTAIN IS CERTAIN TO PROVIDE ENDLESS DELIGHT

AND YOU WILL FIND YOURSELF THINKING OVER
MANY GARDEN PROBLEMS AT THE WATERSIDE

AN OCCASIONAL CLEAN OUT SHOULD PREVENT UNPLEASANT SMELLS

BUT INCORRECT STOCKING CAN UPSET THE BALANCE OF YOUR WATER

YOU WILL BE SURPRISED BY THE WILD BIRDS
THAT WILL APPEAR IN YOUR GARDEN

ONE THING IS CERTAIN —

YOU WILL FIND THE PEACE AND TRANQUILLITY OF WATER
AN ALMOST IRRESISTIBLE ATTRACTION

A LATIN PRIMER

HORIZONTALIS   DEPRESSUS

DISSECTUM   PANICULATA

SPECTABILIS   HORRIDUS

BUXIFOLIUS   FILIFORMIS

WILLIAMSII   CARNIA

ARGENTEA VULGARIS

FRUTICANS   PYRAMIDALIS

PUNGENS PROSTRATUM

ROBINIA FLORIBUNDA

RADIATA NEGLECTUS

FRAGRANS TORTUOSA

FLAVA SUPERBA

ARGUTIFOLIUS   FISTULOSIS

ALPESTRIS LAXIFOLIUS

MONSTROSA IMPRESSUS

SISTUS   CURIOSA

OVALIFOLIUM   LONGIFLORA

THE FIRESIDE JUNGLE

INDOOR PLANTS CAN DO MUCH TO IMPROVE THE VISUAL APPEARANCE OF YOUR ROOMS . . . . .

... BUT SPECIMENS SHOULD NEVER BE INTRODUCED
    UNLESS YOU KNOW HOW TO LOOK AFTER THEM

SEE THAT YOUR PETS ARE WELL PROTECTED
BEFORE USING CHEMICAL SPRAYS

OVER WATERING IS A MAIN CAUSE OF PLANT FAILURE —

AND INCORRECT FEEDING CAN
AFFECT THEM ADVERSELY

A SMOKY ATMOSPHERE IS DETRIMENTAL TO POT PLANTS

— WHILST CENTRAL HEATING IS
INCLINED TO LOOSEN THEIR LEAVES

BEWARE OF INTRODUCING PESTS INTO THE HOUSE WITH NEW SPECIMENS ....

AND IF THEY APPEAR — DESTROY THEM AT ONCE

MAKE SURE EACH PLANT IS SUITABLE
FOR THE PLACE WHERE IT IS KEPT

A GARDENER'S CALENDAR

JANUARY

THIS IS THE MOST CONVENIENT TIME TO WORK OUT YOUR PLANS FOR THE YEAR

LOOK FOR SOME OUT-OF-THE-WAY CORNER

AND START YOUR COMPOST HEAP

IF YOUR FISH POOL IS COVERED WITH ICE...

MAKE A HOLE IN IT

KEEP AN EYE OPEN FOR PESTS

FEBRUARY

THIS IS OFTEN A WET MONTH SO SPIKE YOUR LAWNS
ALL OVER TO IMPROVE DRAINAGE

MAKE A NOTE OF PLACES WHERE PATHS HAVE BECOME SLIPPERY

GO OUT AND REPAIR THEM BEFORE THEY CAUSE TROUBLE

YOUR SNOWDROPS WILL BE LOOKING THEIR BEST NOW

PLANT ROSE TREES IN A SUNNY PART OF THE GARDEN

MAKE SURE YOUR GERANIUMS HAVE NOT DAMPED OFF

MARCH

GIVE SUPPORT TO ANYTHING DISTURBED BY THE WIND

REPAIR ANYTHING LIFTED BY FROST

LOOK OUT FOR DAMAGE BY HAIL

FILL IDLE HOURS BY MAKING YOUR OWN RUSTIC SEAT

USE IT WHEN YOU WANT TO RELAX

BURN ALL YOUR GARDEN RUBBISH

APRIL

YOUR LAWN WILL HAVE STARTED TO GROW NOW

GET YOUR MOWER OUT OF THE SHED

TRY TO PUT THE OTHER THINGS BACK

START UP THE ENGINE

TRY TO REPAIR IT

GET YOUR SCYTHE OUT OF THE SHED

MAY

THE BIRDS WILL BE A DELIGHT THIS MONTH

PROVIDE THEM WITH PLENTY OF NESTING PLACES

ON NO ACCOUNT
DISTURB THE YOUNG

REMOVE PLANTS FROM ROCKERY AFTER FLOWERING AND SPLIT THEM UP

HAND POLLENATE YOUR FRUIT TREES

DRESS WITH CALOMINE LOTION AND GET TO BED

JUNE

APHIS, MILLIPEDES, WEEVILS, SCAB, BLACKLEG, SAWFLY, THRIPS,
PEA MOTHS, MEALY BUGS AND OTHER PESTS WILL BE ACTIVE

MAKE A CAREFUL STUDY OF THESE CREATURES

AND USE EVERY MEANS TO COMBAT THEM

THERE ARE MANY POTENT CHEMICALS ON THE MARKET

BUT PRIVATE THEORIES ARE OFTEN PREFERED

FIND OUT WHY YOUR MOWER HAS NOT BEEN RETURNED

JULY

DROUGHT IN THE GARDEN CAN BE A SERIOUS PROBLEM THIS MONTH

SMALL AMOUNTS OF LIQUID WILL MERELY BRING ROOTS TO THE SURFACE

BUT IT IS AN OFFENCE TO USE A HOSEPIPE
WITHOUT PERMISSION FROM THE LOCAL AUTHORITY

BREAK UP THE HARD SOIL AROUND PLANTS

AND DO EVERYTHING POSSIBLE TO PROVIDE MOISTURE....

THEN GET UNDER COVER BEFORE YOU ARE STRUCK BY
LIGHTNING

AUGUST

AN ALL-OUT EFFORT WILL BE NEEDED TO KEEP CONTROL NOW.
YOU SHOULD NOT HAVE BOOKED YOUR HOLIDAY THIS MONTH

TRY TO FIND A FRIEND WHO WILL KEEP AN EYE
ON THINGS WHILE YOU ARE AWAY

ON NO ACCOUNT LET THE NEIGHBOUR'S DOG SEE YOU GO

DON'T LEAVE PRODUCE BEHIND YOU TO PERISH

ONCE YOU ARE AWAY — RELAX COMPLETELY

YOU'LL NEED ALL YOUR ENERGY WHEN YOU GET HOME

SEPTEMBER

ALL THE FAMILIAR SIGNS OF HARVEST ARE WITH US ONCE MORE

LIFT YOUR MAIN CROP OF POTATOES

TAKE CARE NOT TO BRUISE RIPE FRUIT

ATTEND TO WALL CLIMBERS

CLEAR OUT EXHAUSTED ANNUALS

DISPOSE OF UNPRODUCTIVE FRUIT TREES

OCTOBER

BRUSH ALL LEAVES INTO A NEAT PILE TO ROT.
THEY WILL MAKE VALUABLE PLANT FOOD

WATCH THEM BLOW ALL OVER THE GARDEN AGAIN

SWEEP THEM UP AND SET FIRE TO THEM

TRY TO EXTINGUISH THE POTTING SHED

BRUSH WOOD ASH INTO A NEAT PILE

— IT WILL MAKE VALUABLE PLANT FOOD

WATCH IT BLOW ALL OVER THE GARDEN AGAIN

NOVEMBER

YOUR LAWN WILL HAVE STOPPED GROWING NOW

YOUR MOWER WILL BE RETURNED...

AND YOUR NEIGHBOUR WILL BORROW IT

PUT DOWN CLOCHES TO PROVIDE PROTECTION FROM WORSENING WEATHER

EXAMINE STORED VEGETABLES AND THROW OUT
THOSE WHICH SHOW SIGNS OF ROTTING

BEWARE OF UNEXPLODED FIREWORKS WHEN BURNING RUBBISH

DECEMBER

NEGLECT OF THE GARDEN NOW WILL MEAN HARD WORK
NEXT SEASON — SO KEEP AT IT

DON'T FORGET THE BIRDS — THEY ARE HAVING A HARD TIME OF IT

THE FESTIVE SEASON BRINGS IT'S OWN
INTERESTING LITTLE CHORES...

... AND WELL EARNED REWARDS

THE SNOW WILL BE DEEP NOW ....

.....GET OUT INTO THE GARDEN.....

LIE DOWN — HAVE A REST